Granny Kayla's Guerrilla Gardening Tips

Kayla Starr

Deep Roots Publishing

SEBASTIAN, FLORIDA

Deep Roots Publishing

11155 Roseland Road

Sebastian, Florida 32958

Ordering Information:

Quantity sales. Special discounts are available on quantity purchases by corporations, associations, and others. For details, contact the "Special Sales Department" at the address above.

ISBN: 978-1-7366411-4-9

Contents

INTRODUCTION....................4
GUERRILLA GARDENING....................7
WHERE TO START?....................17
SOIL vs DIRT....................19
COMPOST or BLACK GOLD!....................27
TOOLS....................33
BUILDING YOUR GARDEN BEDS....................34
Amending Your Soil....................35
MULCHING....................40
WATER....................43
WHAT TO PLANT WHERE AND WHEN....................46
COMPANION PLANTING....................50
OKAY, LET'S GET PLANTING!....................55
Peas....................55
Lettuce, Spinach, Bok Choy, Arugula....................57
Brassicas....................58
Garlic, Leeks, Onions....................58
Carrots....................60
Beets and Chard....................61
Green Beans....................62

Tomatoes....63

Cucumbers....65

Squash and Melons....65

Corn....66

Basil....67

Potatoes....68

Culinary and Medicinal Herbs....69

CREEPY CRAWLIES....71

Prevention....72

Cures....73

Beneficial Critters....77

WINTER GROWING....79

TO SUMMARIZE....80

CHAPTER 1

INTRODUCTION

I’m writing this little book at the over-ripe age of 82, to share what I’ve learned growing food and herbs for half a century. Years of experience in any field teaches what works and what doesn’t by trial and error. Indolence inspires ways to make short work of one's efforts. Passion motivates to keep up the good efforts. Joy in the process and the results are the welcome rewards of these efforts.

This book is by no means a comprehensive guide to gardening. Many books already do this…. my go-to garden book being John Jevons: “How to Grow More Vegetables”. This book is more about my own experiences and ideas about growing our own food.

Those who know how to grow food have developed survivor skills that will serve humanity well with the coming Earth changes - as our climate shifts from relative stability to disruptive disequilibrium. Food growing is a radical act. It helps reduce carbon emissions caused by shipping food long distances to our grocery stores in trucks spewing carbon exhaust traveling up and down our highways from many miles distant to our dinner tables. Eating food grown in healthy soil in our backyards is healthier, tastier and kinder to our planet. When we grow food, we are 'giving back', tending to Mother Earth, feeding the soil, making use of the fertility we create to feed ourselves, our family and friends.

There is great personal benefit to being outside in fresh air, in warm sunshine and gray chill rain, with feet on the earth, with hands in the soil, birthing and nurturing our own food. Food growing benefits our bodies as we work outside, it feeds our souls to be in close relationship to the land and the plants. Tending my garden calms me, centers me, connects me to Nature, brings peace to my often agitated mind. I am never in a bad mood when I'm gardening. I've read that the human body produces more endorphins when it is touching the Earth.

GUERRILLA GARDENING

What is "guerrilla gardening"? Usually, it means gardening on land that you do not own. However, the definition also includes gardening with a political purpose, seeking to make change by using food growing as a form of protest or direct action.

Food production in this country has been hijacked by powerful corporations that now dominate agriculture and put profits over people and our environment. Growing our own food counters some of the evils of

Big Agribusiness, making us less dependent on corporations, uses fewer scarce resources, avoids using poisons on our food supply, puts carbon back in the ground instead of into our atmosphere, and sets an example for others to take back our food system. Food growing is a way of connecting with our friends and neighbors, sharing advice and trading produce.

I always have extra lettuce and kale and cucumbers to give away, and appreciate getting squash and berries from my neighbors who have excess from their gardens. Then there's the satisfaction of opening a jar of pesto, a bag of frozen broccoli or a jar of dried tomatoes in the dark of winter, that came from your garden the summer before.

Growing our own food has another benefit as well. Where there is food being produced, there are less lawns! Though pretty to look at, lawns are seriously bad for the environment. They are a poor use scarce resources: water, arable land, fertilizer, time and e ort to keep them mowed, land that could be used to feed people, oh and then there's the poisonous herbicides that lawns require to keep the weeds down, that kill beneficial insects and that drain into our waterways. When I see a wide green lawn, I think of the wasted precious water used to keep it green; I think of the gas powered lawn mowers used to keep it trim; I think of the wasted human labor used to maintain it; I think of the fruit and nut trees, the berries and veggies that could be there instead! Down with lawns!

Down with lawns!

When I started gardening way back in the 1970s, I got two books from my local library in Los Angeles, CA: John Jevons; "How to Grow More Vegetables" and a little paperback by Ruth Stout: "Gardening from the Couch". These are the only two books I have ever read on gardening. I have never taken a class on how to grow food. Instead, I made it a point to talk to other local food gardeners to learn about methods - what does and doesn't work in my locality.

I started growing food for practical reasons in Los Angeles when I was raising my two toddler daughters. My husband was training to become a doctor, and we were living on a meager income. Growing food was a way to keep within a tight budget and provide healthy food for my family. We rented and moved often - every 1-4 years and I found myself making small veggie gardens wherever we lived. Each location offered different growing conditions in terms of soil health, sunshine, and access to water. Of course, the mild sunny climate in L. A. in the early 70's was a big asset. Temperatures were always in the range of 50 to 85 degrees with plenty of sunshine year round. When I moved to Southern Oregon 40 years ago, it was a new ball game.

My first 10 years in Oregon I lived in Takilma, a tiny community of back-to-landers settled in the mountains at the headwaters of the Illinois River near Cave Junction. I was fortunate to start out on a commune with experienced home growers to learn from. We have real seasons here in Southern Oregon, including freezing temps possible from late October through April, unlike Southern California, so learning what to plant when was all new for me. My food growing neighbors were happy to show me the hows and why's.

The last three years, I have been growing food at my own little place in Talent, just outside of Ashland, Oregon. The growing season is between March and October here. Some vegetables can winter over, so as I write this in February, I am able to go outside and dig up leeks I planted almost a year ago, carrots, beets, kale and collard greens that were planted late last summer. Over the summer, I grew lettuce, peas, spinach, broccoli, eggplant, carrots, tomatoes, leeks, potatoes, green beans, ground cherries, spinach, cucumbers, kale, chard, collards, green onion, beets, strawberries, blueberries, raspberries, basil, parsley, comfrey, chives, thyme, cilantro, oregano, tarragon, lemon balm, dill, three varieties of mint. And a couple of cannabis plants! All this grew in 3 garden beds - about 8 feet long and several large pots and boxes and grow bags. My property is blessed with lots of marionberry vines. I planted strawberries, raspberries and blueberries which all did poorly last year, so the marionberries were much appreciated! I have NEVER succeeded with strawberries, ever, anywhere! Yet, I keep trying year after year.

Flowers are not my specialty, though I love to have them around. I did have some success last season with sweet peas, iris, cosmos, roses, zinnias, yarrow, honeysuckle, jasmine, marigolds, petunias, pansies, tulips, gladiolas, clematis, and Columbine. The flowers did bloom, but never as big and bright as flowers I see in my neighbors' yards. I can't really explain why I tend to do poorly with most flowers and berries, so this book will offer little help with these plants.

I take pride in the produce I nurtured in my garden over the last 6 months. I have preserved (canned, dried, or frozen) for this winter:

Blueberries, marionberries, peaches that I picked at a nearby organic orchard, green beans, tomatoes, (dried, frozen canned, made into sauce, and soup), peas, pesto, pickles, broccoli, oregano, dill, basil, tarragon, comfrey, parsley, mints, lemon balm - and cannabis! And in the dark of winter, there are still some carrots, beets, kale, collards, chives, leeks to harvest. None of this was here when I moved here 3 years ago, except the marionberries and 2 rose bushes.

EAT LESS FROM A BOX
This is how we create
significant change
AND MORE FROM
THE EARTH
made with mematic

MY GUIDING GARDEN PRINCIPLES

- Use what you have on hand! (for compost, mulch, fertilizer, trellises, and building raised beds.
- Minimize buying stu from big corporations, especially plastic and artificial chemicals. Reduce, Reuse, Repurpose, Repair, Be Creative.
- Start small, choosing what's easiest first, what you really enjoy eating, what grows well in your climate. Cultivate small successes first.

- Share your abundance with your neighbors, friends and family. Sharing your skills and your produce builds community and furthers the movement for sustainable living.
- Learn to tune into your garden with your intuition and the plants will tell you what they need.
- Build fertile soil.
- Conserve water.
- Replace lawns with fruits and veggies.

WHERE TO START?

Ask yourself if you will be around enough during the growing season to tend to your garden at least every other day. Do you have a neighbor nearby to water and harvest when you do go away for several days. In temperate climates you can usually leave the garden untended for 2-3 days if temperatures will be under 90 degrees. If you travel for weeks at a time during the growing season, your garden will probably not fare well. Learning from other gardeners in my area was the often the most useful information, while it also served to create and enhance community connections. Having good connections with your neighbors is a valuable asset, especially when hard times hit. Three years ago, our area was devastated by a wildfire that drove most of the town away and cut off water and electricity for 2 weeks. One neighbor managed to stay, knew I had crops growing and needing water. They took it upon themselves to kindly carry several gallons of water to my potted plants and kept everything alive, till I could return.

Decide where to put your garden. Most vegetables require 8 hours of sun daily. Most need watering every other day during warm weather. Many crops can be planted in large pots, but potted plants need more frequent watering. Some crops - lettuce, spinach, peas, cilantro, kale, collards, parsley - do well with only half a day of sunshine - morning sun is better for these plants.

Decide what you want to grow. Best to start small with 3 - 6 crops, so you can learn what works best for you. Consider what are your favorite things to eat, what is easier to grow, what sun and water conditions are in your garden, how much time you want to devote to your garden. Find out if you have neighbors or friends nearby who grow food. Ask them what works for them.

SOIL vs DIRT

The foundation of your garden is your soil. Without good soil, you will not get good results. I don't call it 'dirt' because the definition of dirt is "a filthy substance such as mud, dust, or grime; something worthless". Soil is a sweet smelling fertile medium that feeds and supports your plants. Vegetables do best in soil that is at least 10 - 12 inches deep, flu y and full of organic materials. Not too acid or alkali.

In most gardens, your soil will need to be conditioned to create this. In my gardens in California and S. Oregon, I have had heavy clay, acid-y soils . In desert and coastal areas, the soil is sandy and alkaline. In conifer forest areas, your soil may be too acidic for most crops.

Once you've chosen your best sunny area close to a watering source, you will dig into your soil to determine what supplements will be needed to create the best foundation for the roots of your plants. In clay soils, you will need to add more organic matter - compost, coconut coir, biochar, rice hulls, worms, animal or green manure.

GOOD CARBON/BAD CARBON

I'm sure that most of you are painfully aware of the crisis we are facing on this planet due to carbon that is spewing into our atmosphere from burning fossil fuels.

For over 25 years, scientists have been warning about the destructive effects of excess carbon in the air. Not only are temperatures rising, sea water is warming, destroying habitat for fish, all over the planet, coral reefs are dying from this heating, sea levels are rising creating more and more need for people to move inland - climate migration. Animal and plant species are going extinct at such a rate, science is calling this the Sixth Major Extinction Event on this planet.

Food crops are withering in the heat, forests are burning out of control, cities are flooding, glaciers are melting, storms are increasingly severe. The ocean current in the Atlantic is slowing. The Gulf Stream brings heat to Europe. As it flows northward and cools, the water mass becomes heavier. The sinking of water near Greenland pulls water from elsewhere in the Atlantic Ocean and the cycle repeats. Too much fresh water from melting glaciers and the Greenland ice sheet dilutes the saltiness of the water, preventing it from sinking, and weakens it. A weaker conveyor belt transports less heat northward and also enables less heavy water to reach Greenland, which further weakens the conveyor belt's strength. Once it reaches the tipping point, it shuts down quickly.

The delicate balance of all life support systems on this planet is failing.

Government, industry, climate scientists and environmental activists have been meeting for over two decades to address this threat to all life on the planet. Hundreds of books and articles are written, legislation to address this life-threatening crisis languishes in legislatures around the world. Dozens of environmental organizations are working hard every day to slow the destruction. Perhaps you've heard and even supported some of these groups. Extinction Rebellion, Rainforest Action network, GreenPeace, Climate Justice Alliance, Sunrise Movement, The Climate Emergency Fund.etc. are supporting climate solutions, organizing protests, and blockading fossil fuel plants, pipelines, logging old growth forests.

Proposed solutions abound. Switch to electric cars, build more wind and solar power, insulate our buildings, recycle, drive less, fly less, buy less, reproduce less. The military is by far the biggest producer of carbon, so the anti-war movement tries to curb the war machine. None of these solutions are being applied at a scale that can make a difference, so far. And many of them rely on resource extraction and manufacturing methods that actually add to the problem.

Still, the US - the biggest producer of greenhouse gasses - continues to award more permits to "drill, baby, drill - to oil, coal and gas producers. Both Democrats and Republicans rely on contributions from the fossil fuel and weapons producers, so they are not willing to call a halt.

Legislative proposals die in Congress every year. And of course, Europe, China, India, Russia, the other major contributors to the problem, are on the same suicidal path.

Every year, more carbon is released into the atmosphere, storms are worse, wildfires burn down our towns, crops fail, species go extinct. Many of us are feeling deeply frightened and discouraged. We vote for climate protection candidates, we are recycling, buying cars that use less gasoline, curtailing plane trips, moving our money to banks that don't support oil companies, meeting with our legislators, attending marches and demonstrations.

My own approach nowadays is using creative, non-violent civil disobedience to stop business as usual at financial institutions that fund fossil fuel and weapons companies, blockading fossil fuel installations, sitting in at the governor's office to pressure her to stop gas pipelines proposed to cross our state. We bring giant puppets, banners, street murals, dance and music to the streets to attract attention to our efforts and focus on beauty and life-affirming images in our movements. We've seen some success, stopping more nuclear power plants from being built, cancelling a pipeline here and there, halting the destruction of an occasional old growth forest…..Yet, every year, more carbon is released into the atmosphere. It keeps getting worse.

So, why are we talking about this here in a little backyard gardening manual? I bring this into our awareness because we actually can make a small contribution to reducing carbon in the atmosphere in our own little gardens. This solution, recognized by science, is called sequestering carbon in the soil.

Soils are made in part of broken-down plant matter. This means they contain a lot of carbon that those plants took in from the atmosphere while they were alive. Soils can store or "sequester" this carbon for a very long time. If not for soil, this carbon would return to the atmosphere as carbon dioxide (CO_2), the main cause of climate destruction.

Over the past 12,000 years, the growth of farmland has released about 110 billion metric tons of carbon from the top layer of soil—roughly equivalent to 80 years' worth of present-day U.S. emissions. The question is: Can this trend be reversed at the global scale as part of a strategy to help fight climate change? Scientists have estimated that soils—mostly, agricultural ones—could sequester over a billion additional tons of carbon each year.[4] This has led policymakers to increasingly look to soil-based carbon sequestration as a "negative emissions" technology—that is, one that removes CO_2 from the air and stores it somewhere it can't easily escape.

Cropland, which takes up 10% of the Earth's land, is a major target for soil-based carbon sequestration. Farmers can add more carbon to agricultural soils by planting certain kinds of crops. For example, perennial crops, which do not die off every year, grow deep roots that help soils store more carbon. “Cover crops” like clover, beans and peas, planted after the main crop is harvested, help soils take in carbon year-round, and can be plowed under the ground as “green manure” that adds more carbon to the soil. Farmers can also do less intensive tilling. By breaking up the soil, tilling prepares land for new crops and helps control weeds, but also releases a lot of stored carbon.

Farming/gardening practices that store more carbon improves soil health and food production. Ultimately, scientists say soil-based carbon sequestration, like other negative emissions technologies, can help fight climate change, However, to stop global warming, these efforts to store carbon must be coupled with drastic cuts in greenhouse gas emissions.

In the meantime, we individual back yard gardeners can set an example for our neighbors by putting as much carbon back into our soils as possible. We do this by composting our kitchen and yard waste. All those buckets of compost are keeping CO2 out of trash piles and land fill. Some also add carbon to their backyard garden soil by setting up grey water systems, diverting kitchen, shower and laundry water out of our sewer systems and into our gardens. Some even save their urine and use it in the garden. All these practices enrich our gardens while reducing the amount to carbon that ends up in the atmosphere. You will see more about how to make compost later in this little book.

U.S; the land of socialized losses and privatized profits. How long will taxpayers be willing to bale out the billionaires?

COMPOST or BLACK GOLD!

I am passionate about composting. Compost uses food and yard waste to create enriched, fertile soil for your garden. It keeps carbon in the ground, it saves money as you won't need to buy as much manure and soil conditioners. You use your food scraps, weeds and trimmings, grass clippings and fallen leaves to make rich black fluffy organic soil. It seems like magic to me, that garbage can so easily be transformed in a few months to this priceless gift for your garden. What a satisfying feeling to be re-using what would otherwise go into landfill, saving money at the garden store, while adding the perfect fertilizer and conditioner to enrich your garden beds.

Here's how it's done:

Build yourself a square bin or two - about 3 feet square each, with wooden slats or chicken wire sides, so air can flow through. I use pallets as I'm nearly hopeless with carpentry tools. A friend has said that if it can't be fixed or made with string, WD-40 or duct tape, I need to call in the experts!

I just scavenge 4 smaller sized pallets, stand them on end and tie them together to form a square box and place them on bare ground not too far from the kitchen door, where it will get sun and fresh air, and not too far from the garden. I tie them together with used nylon baling twine that comes omy straw bales. This cord is very strong and durable, lasting in all weather conditions for many years. The front entrance is tied in bows on one side, so it can be opened up like a gate to access the compost pile. This method is completely free, uses only recycled materials and takes less than an hour to 'build'. Or if you're good with saws, drills, hammers etc, you can design and build your compost bins out of used lumber. Be sure to leave gaps between the slats so air can get in. Many designs can be easily found on YouTube. Ideally, if you have room, build 2 boxes side by side. Here's why: your compost needs to have air and some moisture to break down into good soil. So it needs to be lifted and turned every two weeks or so. Turning it into the second bin helps to keep it aerated. If you have only one bin, you can still lift and turn your pile from side to side in the same bin every few weeks. A good digging fork is the only tool needed.

So, you start with soil on the bottom of your bin, add a layer two to four inches deep of leaves, straw or weeds. then start bringing out your kitchen compost bucket, called the 'green' layer, and dump that on top. Cover each layer of kitchen compost with leaves or straw or grass clippings or weeds. This is called the Brown layer. I try to do a 2-3 inch layer of kitchen waste, then 3 - 4 inches of brown stuff . About every two weeks, put in a couple of shovels full of soil to add the microbes that live in your soil which helps break down your food scraps into compost. Once a month, sprinkle a shovel-full of manure to add nitrogen that will heat up the pile and make it break down faster. Worms are your good friends in the garden. Add "red wigglers" to your compost pile. You can get a shovel full of worms from a neighbor who grows food/compost or from the soil in your garden beds, or from your garden store. In the summer, if the pile becomes dry, add a bucket of water occasionally to keep it moist. Every week or two, take a digging fork or shovel and turn the compost so that the layers get air and mix together. In about 2-3 months, you will have finished compost which smell kind of sweet and looks dark brown/black, with no sign of the egg shells, coffee grounds, celery stalks, bread crusts, etc. that you started with. Put your finished compost into buckets or wheelbarrows to take to the garden. Stir it into your garden beds before planting to condition and feed your soil, and use it as mulch on top of the soil around growing plants.

What goes into your kitchen compost bucket? All fruit and veggie scraps, eggs, egg shells, bread, pasta, whatever is scraped off of your dinner plates, except large bones. I also avoid putting corn cobs and avocado seeds and skins, as these take forever to break down into compost. Most composters say don't put meat scraps into the compost as that can attract rodents, flies, etc.

The more often you turn your pile, the sooner it will be ready to use in the garden. My 80 year old back limits the frequency I get around to turning my pile so it's often just once a month here, which makes for a slower pace to complete the process. The organic matter breaks down from the work of soil microbes, worms and heat that builds up as it works. This is why you need the pile to be about 3 feet square, so it can build up the heat that helps transform your garbage into "Black Gold". Ideally you will have enough finished compost to make a layer 2 inches thick in your grow areas.

My Way   Cadillac of Compost Bins

If you have neighbors in the area who keep chickens, horses or sheep, see if they'd like someone to take away their old animal bedding. This is terrific for your compost pile or as mulch as it's part straw and part manure. As the mulch slowly breaks down over the winter, it's adding nitrogen to your soil. When planting time comes around in early spring, all you need to do is move the mulch out of the way, use your trowel to dig a hole about 6 inches deep, add some composted chicken manure and bone or fish meal, and stir well into the soil, then plant your baby plant starts above the fertilizer with a 1-2 inch layer of soil between the manure and the roots of your plant. No weeding or digging in hard compacted soil will be needed. So easy and your veggies are o   to a great start in fertile soil. The tender roots of your plant starts can burn if they come in direct contact with manure, so be sure the scoop of manure is deeper and mixed in well in your garden soil.

In the Spring, my routine is to rake to the edges of my garden beds the leaf mulch that has fed my soil and kept weeds at bay all winter. Then I add compost, organic composted chicken manure, and powdered bone meal. Dig it all in well, and your beds are then ready to support your plant. If your beds have been well conditioned in previous years, you may only need to use a hand trowel to make holes for your plants and add a half cup of chicken manure in the bottom of the hole then place your plants, press into the soil, and water them in.

TOOLS

Here are some items you will need to purchase or borrow or get donated. You need a good shovel, a digging fork, a rake, a couple of trowels, a pruning clipper and a pruning saw. Most gardeners use hoes also, but since I mulch heavily I don't need a hoe to remove weeds. You will also need stakes and cages to hold up vining plants such as tomatoes, climbing beans, peas and cucumbers. I use mostly bamboo poles to stake my plants that I have access to from a friend who grows bamboo. You can also use trimmed tree branches, wooden poles and berry vine trimmings to make cages and trellises to support your plants. Be creative, scavenge! You will want some plastic netting to keep birds from feasting on your baby sprouts and ripe berries. You will use nylon, jute or hemp string to train your vining plants. I also use a product that I have to purchase called Row Cover which protects young plants from mild frosts and certain garden pests. It is like very thin cloth but is permeable to water, keeps the temperature about 5 degrees warmer inside, keeps out bugs, and reduces water evaporation. It can be reused for up to 5 seasons if you are careful not to tear it.

BUILDING YOUR GARDEN BEDS

Walk around your land in mid-morning and late afternoon to see where the sun is most of the day. That's where you want your veggies to grow. Most veggies need at least 8 hours of sun to grow and produce well. Also, that area needs to be accessible to your hose faucets for watering.

For non-desert areas, raised beds are the best. I like my garden beds to be about 4 feet wide. Build your beds 2 - 3 feet apart so you can get in there with your garden cart and buckets to work on your beds. If you are tall, with long arms, you can go up to 5 feet in width. You can build your beds any length from square to up to 30 feet long.

You can use plywood that is at least 8 inches wide for the sides, or 2 x 8 foot lengths of lumber, or pile up rocks to a height of 8 inches, or you can use concrete blocks for the sides of your garden bed. Use recycled wood rather than purchasing new wood if possible. Be creative. I've seen people using old bookcases and drawers for garden beds. I've used milk crates, grow bags, even strong cardboard boxes, lining the sides with used plastic bags. I use old carpets cut in 3 foot wide strips and or large cardboard boxes on the paths between my beds to keep weeds down.

Amending Your Soil

I like composted chicken manure for the nitrogen fertilizer that plants need for green foliage growth. I add bone meal or fish meal (for potassium) which is food for flowering and fruiting, and wood ashes (potash) from my friend's wood stove for strong root growth. If you have access to biochar and worm castings, those are terrific additions to your soil. You can also use llama, alpaca, sheep, horse or cow manure instead of chicken manure. These are less intense than the chicken poop, so you need to double the amount used.

Biochar is made by burning wood scraps in a low oxygen (pyrolytic) situation which limits the release of carbon in the atmosphere and sequesters it for use in creating more fertile soil. In addition to improving soil quality, converting biomass to biochar can prevent carbon emissions from reaching the atmosphere. With pyrolysis, the carbon is locked in a stable form that resists decay, sequestering it for hundreds of years. Biochar remains in the ground for centuries, slowing the growth of greenhouse gasses, improving water quality, and increasing soil fertility.

Next, determine if your soil needs to be flu ed up with organic matter such as coconut coir or rice hulls. If you take a fistful of damp soil and squeeze it in your hand and it holds its shape in a hard clump, then it needs some amending to flu it up, to encourage easy root growth and holding moisture. I don't recommend using peat moss. This product is found in most potting soils you buy. Peat moss forms very slowly in cool wetlands as sphagnum moss decays. The bogs are called "carbon sinks" due to the massive amounts of carbon they store—far more than trees. When peat moss is harvested, carbon dioxide is released, contributing to climate change. Coconut coir is one of the most e ective growing media for water retention. It can absorb up to 10 times its weight in water, meaning the roots of your plants will never get dehydrated. There's also a lot of growing media for roots to work through, promoting healthy root development. Coconut coir, unlike peat moss, which breaks down more rapidly, keeps lightening your soil for many years. It's also a repurposed waste product from a renewable resource, unlike the peat bogs where they harvest peat moss. It's made from coconut husks and is in plentiful supply. It's insect neutral: Most garden pests do not enjoy settling in coconut coir, making it yet another line of defense in the pest management e orts for your garden.

You want to add the equivalent of about 4 inches total of all these soil amendments for a garden bed composed of top soil, which is at least 8 inches deep. One fourth of the amendments will be your manure and fertilizer, 1/2 will be soil lighteners, ¼ should be compost. My favorite manure to use is composted organic chicken poop. I do have to buy it in bags at the store since I currently don't have access to farms nearby or a truck to transport it. In the past, when I lived with horses, I have used horse poop. I used alpaca poop when I lived next door to an alpaca farm. If you have access to animal bedding - straw mixed with droppings of chicken, rabbit, horse, alpacas, etc, that's the best. You will be making friends with farming neighbors, helping them get rid of excess bedding and giving your soil terrific organic amendments. Use your shovel to dig these ingredients down into your planting beds, then rake the bed smooth to be ready to host your plants and seeds. Be sure to mix these fertilizers into your topsoil really well before planting.

Preparing your garden beds is the only heavy work you will need to do in starting your garden the first year. Building your beds, turning and mixing the soil and amendments thoroughly creates the foundation that is essential for healthy productive plants. If you mulch your beds thickly with leaves or straw at the end of your growing season, in subsequent seasons, there will be no more turning tons of soil ever again.

During the growing season, layer more compost around the roots - not up against the stems, and lots of mulch to keep feeding the plants as they grow. When the mulch is at least 4 inches thick, you will greatly reduce weeds growing in your garden beds. The occasional weed that pokes through, will be easy to pull and add to your compost bin. Different veggies will need different amounts of nutrients, which will be discussed later.

At the end of the season, chop up some of the spent veggie greens and stems and leave on the bed, then cover with 4-6 inches of maple leaves when they fall in November. If you don't have access to maple trees, you can use straw. This way, you will have only a few weeds to pull when you go out next spring to start your new growing season. You can just push the composting leaves aside, dig a small hole, stir in a trowel full of fertilizer/compost, cover with an inch or 2 of soil and place your baby plant in the hole. Then cover it lightly with soil, and keep the mulch a few inches away from the stem of your baby plant, so the soil around its roots will warm and the stem will be free to grow. Always gently water in your new plantings with a sprinkling can or hose to help the roots get established.

MULCHING

If you don't feel like pulling weeds all summer long; if you'd prefer to save water in your garden; if you want to effortlessly feed your soil year-round then you

will want to mulch your garden beds. Mulch is a blanket of organic material laid on top of your soil around your plants. Mulch holds moisture in the soil that would otherwise evaporate in hot weather.
If you keep your layer of mulch 4-6 inches deep, 95 percent of weed seeds will never see the light of day. And while it is sitting on your soil, it slowly breaks down into compost, feeding the roots of your plants. The best mulch in the summertime is straw. It's lightweight, breaks down slowly, easy to apply to your garden beds and fairly inexpensive to buy.

A bale or 2 of straw is the best investment you can make to have a successful, easy to care for, garden. Don't use hay as it has grass and weed seeds which will contaminate your garden beds. Don't use wood chips as they are too acidic for your veggies. In the winter, I use maple leaves that fall from the trees in my next-door neighbor's yard. Maple is better than other leaves because it's low in acid. You can also mulch your potted plants and flower beds with straw to free yourself from constant weed pulling all summer long. I learned about mulching from a book by Ruth Stout called "Gardening From Your Couch." It's really true that it seriously cuts down on the task of weeding, while adding nourishment to your soil.

WATER

There is no exact formula for how much water to give your veggie garden. It depends on air temperature, type of watering system you are using, soil condition, if you are using thick mulch, and particular vegetable requirements. Of course when it's really hot - over 90 degrees - your plants will need more water - once a day; if the temps are low 60's, you may need to water just once a week. The best way to learn how much water is needed is to stick your finger into your soil an hour after watering and if it is moist at least 2 inches down, that's enough. If it's muddy, that's too much. If it's dry, you need to water more. Sandy soils need more water; clay soils, less. The mistake I see with most beginner gardeners is not watering long enough to get the moisture down to the roots of your plants. Surface watering keeps your roots shallow and more susceptible to problems. Deep roots do better than shallow roots as they have more access to the nutrients in your soil and make for stronger plants, able to withstand heat and garden pests. If water pools on top of your garden beds and does not penetrate within a few minutes of being watered, the soil is too compacted and/or you over watered. Your plants won't grow well in muddy/wet soil as they need some air pockets in the ground so the roots don't drown.

If you are overhead watering with a sprinkler or hand-held hose, you will need to use more water for longer times since up to 1/3 of the water will evaporate into the air. If you have a drip system set up, where the water is applied directly onto the soil around the plants, you will conserve water, especially if your plants are well mulched. Many gardeners with small gardens actually prefer to hand water with a garden hose if they have the time for it, as they become more observant and connected to their plants that way.

For my garden which is watered with an oscillating sprinkler, and contains 4 4x8 mulched beds, in mid-summer when it's in the low 90's, I water every other day for 1-2 hours. My sprinkler is on a timer set for 1.5 hours every other day for most of the summer. Early morning watering is best as there is less water evaporation when the air is cool, and the plants will dry out during the heat of the day, thus being less susceptible to garden pests. Which like to come out feast at night. If you are fortunate to have a drip watering system and your plants are well-mulched, you may only need to water every 3rd day for 1-2 hours or so, depending on how fast the water is being delivered.

The thing with drip systems covered with mulch, you have to keep a close eye out for leaks and blockages as the little tubes and holes can easily spring a leak or get blocked with debris. I cannot offer advice on setting up a drip system or trouble-shooting such a system as I have only a little experience using this watering method. The times I have tried it, I had frequent clogging and leaking.

Some gardeners prefer to hand water everything with a hose if they have time to do that. This way they are communing with their plants and having time to get an intuitive feel for what each plant needs, to see if there are pests threatening them, and feel out when they are ready to harvest. Yes, I do believe that plants communicate with us when we take the time and focus to listen. Hand watering is one way that happens. One thing about hand watering; you need to be sure you are watering long enough for the soil to get moist down to the roots. Many who hand water do not spent the time it takes for the water to get down there and so the roots stay shallow. Shallow roots can't reach the nutrients deeper in the soil and don't give enough structural support to the plants above.

I find myself walking out to the garden most morning, barefooted, feeling into what the plants want that day.

The gardener's intuition is important. You will learn to look at your plants and notice/feel if something doesn't seem quite right, if the leaves are droopy or not thriving, after some experience. Being tuned in psychically to your plants is one of the great gifts of being a food grower. It will come fairly quickly if you stay open and "listen" to your garden.

WHAT TO PLANT WHERE AND WHEN

Ask yourself what vegetables you like best and use most often. Make a list. Now choose up to 8 of these veggies to start out with. Some crops are easier to grow, some more challenging. Choose the easier ones to start with, so you can experience success your first time out. Here is a list of the easier to grow veggies: Lettuce, radish, kale, collards, chard, parsley, cucumbers, green onions, garlic, leeks, tomatoes, green beans, peas, beets, summer squash, mint, oregano.

Harder to grow: Carrots (tricky to germinate from seed), corn (heavy feeder and needs a large area - 4 rows a foot apart - to pollinate properly), broccoli (goes to seed easily with warm weather), cilantro (easily goes to seed), Basil (needs warmth and moisture), celery (needs a lot of water), spinach (goes to seed easily) eggplant and peppers (need lots of warmth).

Now that you have your list of most liked and easier to grow crops, you need to know where and when to plant. Plants that like cooler weather and shade in the afternoons: Peas, spinach, lettuce, arugula and cilantro, can go in areas that get mostly morning sun or partly shaded from trees.

Crops that need heat and lots of sun: Tomatoes, cucumbers, green beans, melons, peppers, eggplant, squashes, basil - all need the soil to be at least 60 degrees in order to grow well and have long sunny days.

I put leeks in my garden in February and harvest them late summer and harvest them all the way to the next spring! I plant my peas, lettuce, cilantro, spinach, and parsley on the side of my house that gets great morning sun and shade in the late afternoon. I start them in late February or early March in S. Oregon. If all goes well, I am eating peas, spinach, parsley and lettuce by May.

I start collards, kale, chard, broccoli, cabbage in March indoors, and more lettuce gets planted where they will get shaded by the brassica leaves as they grow into June/July. I start carrots, beets and onions in April. Plant 4 - 6 lettuces every 2-3 weeks beginning in April until June, then again in August and September.

Plant tomatoes, cucumbers, squash, potatoes, melons and basil in mid to late May, when the soil has warmed and no more freezes are on the horizon. Plant garlic in November or December for harvesting in late June/early July.

Some gardeners plant and harvest by the phases of the moon, in the belief that will make their plants stronger. My style; I watch the weather reports very carefully every day. I plant when the soil will be warm enough to keep the new baby roots happy, when it will not be pouring rain, windy or so hot the new plants will want to keel over and dry up before their roots can drink in moisture from the soil. It takes 48 hours for newly planted roots to begin to use the moisture and fertility in the soil - to get established. When the weather is warm, the best time to put in your seedlings is in the early evening so they can adjust during the night and be ready to face the hot sun the next day. In hot weather I often fluff up the straw mulch so it partly shades the new plants until their roots get established.

Even expert gardeners have some crops that do not do well each season. Reasons can be weather conditions, garden pests, not enough of something the plant needs to thrive. That's where the mystery of the plant and your intuitive connection to your garden comes into play. So plant more of each veggie than you expect to use, knowing that some will likely not make it to maturity. When you have more than you can use, give some away to neighbors, friends, soup kitchens. Further down, I will talk about each of these plants and what they specifically need for best results.

COMPANION PLANTING

Many vegetables thrive better when planted in close proximity to other types of plants. Plants can attract beneficial insects and pollinators, deter pests, and act as insect repellants. They can fend off predators and undesirable wildlife. Raccoons, for instance, dislike the smell of cucumbers.

Plants also play a role in soil fertility by improving the nutrient supply, availability, and uptake from the soil. Interplanting different crops can help mark garden rows and distinguish fast-germinating plants like radishes from slower-germinating plants like carrots. Companion planting can even help suppress weeds.

The classic combination is called Three Sisters, and was used by First Nation gardeners. It involves planting Corn, Green Beans and Squash in the same garden bed. The green beans add nitrogen to the soil, thus feeding the corn which has big nitrogen needs. The squash shades the soil around the corn and beans so they need less water and keeps the weeds down. The beans use the tall strong corn stalks to grow up into the light. All are happier plants in this threesome relationship.

Peas are happier when lettuce, spinach or beets are grown together as pea roots need to be kept cool and moist, and the broad leaves of the lettuce shade the pea roots. Peas do NOT like to be near onions or garlic. Tomatoes and potatoes do not like to grow next to each other. Brassicas (broccoli, kale, collards) need to be planted 18 to 24 inches apart to do their best, so the space in between is perfect for lettuce or spinach in the summer as their broad leaves are taller and give shade to keep cool the lettuce and spinach, slowing them from going to seed in the heat.

Cucumbers, sunflowers, and pole beans: The principle here is the same as for the three sisters: the sunflower supports climbing pole beans, while cucumber vines shield the ground.

Basil and tomatoes: These can be considered "best friends" in the garden. Basil repels thrips and disrupts the habits of the moths that cause tomato hornworms. However, in my experience the basil never does well next to tomatoes as it doesn't get enough sun.

Parsley and tomatoes: Parsley needs less sun and attracts beneficial insects that help keep control of damaging insects that prey on tomato plants.

Sage, with carrots or cabbage. Sage is a proven repellant for carrot flies and cabbage moths.

Some plants benefit almost any plant they are paired with—either by repelling damaging insects or attracting beneficial insects that prey on the bad guys. These champions include:

Nasturtiums: lures hungry caterpillars away from brassicas, including cabbage, broccoli, and kale.

Marigolds: with repel flying, crawling and soil dwelling critters.
Mint: This plant's scent strongly repels aphids, ants, and flea beetles.

Garlic

Garlic: This onion relative has a strong scent that is repugnant to aphids, and repels a variety of mites, moths, and beetles.
Dill: This plant is known to attract ladybugs, which

are voracious eaters of damaging aphids and spider mites.

Borage: attracts bees for pollinating your garden.

Planting flowers and herbs in with your veggies also makes a prettier garden.

OKAY, LET'S GET PLANTING!

I plant most of my veggies in small pots inside next to sunny windows to start out as this keeps them safer from pests as they establish strong roots and stems. The only exceptions are peas and carrots whose seeds I put straight into the ground.

Peas

My first crop in late February/early March is peas. Peas produce from about May into early July in the right location. I soak the seeds overnight in room temp water to soften the outer skin and help them to germinate faster. Peas need a trellis to climb up. Some pea varieties grow to 6 feet tall, some just to 3-4 feet tall. Peas like cool moist soil to grow well, so the west side of your house is the best place for them or somewhere that they will get some shade from afternoon sun. I plant shelling peas, snow peas and sugar snap peas.

First, I build a trellis about 6 feet tall. I use 1 inch diameter bamboo stakes about 6 feet apart and 6-8 inches deep, against a west facing wall. You can also use wood, metal or plastic stakes, whatever is easily at hand. Metal or plastic stakes will last the longest in soil. Bamboo will be good for 3-4 seasons before the bottom will begin to break down in the soil. I tie 8 ft long thin stakes or boards horizontally to the bottom and top of these uprights and then use nylon string going up and down around these horizontals about 2 inches apart so the pea plants can wrap their tendrils around as they grow tall. Then I dig a trench just in front of the trellis about 3 inches deep and dig in some powdered bone or fish meal and stir it in. Then I drop the soaked pea seeds about 1 inch apart into the trench and cover with about 1 inch of soil from the trench. Leave the rest of the dug up soil in front to cover the seedlings later after they are a few inches tall. Then water in the seeds. Cover with row cover to keep hungry birds from going along the row of pea sprouts and pulling them up for their Springtime breakfast. Otherwise, you may lose the whole row of baby pea sprouts to hungry birds.

The peas will sprout in about 10 to 14 days, depending on the warmth of your soil. What a happy sight to see your first little green sprouts coming up. When they are about 2 inches tall, you can remove the row cover as they are now well rooted and can't be easily harvested by the birds. As soon as they are up, I plant spinach and lettuce that have been started from seed in small plant pots inside and are at least 2 inches tall, I put them right in front of the pea row trench. The lettuce leaves keep the soil cooler which keeps your peas producing longer. As the peas grow, add the dug up soil in the trench where you planted the peas. Snow peas ripen first, then sugar snaps, then shelling peas. Pick snow peas when you can see the shapes of their little peas inside; that's when they are the sweetest. Pick the snap peas when the pods are cylindrical in shape, not flat, for the sweetest result. Same for the shelling peas. All three types of peas are excellent for freezing when you have had your fill of their sweet freshness.

Lettuce, Spinach, Bok Choy, Arugula

So many wonderful varieties of lettuce to choose from. I mostly grow butter lettuce and romaine as they are less likely to bolt/go to seed, when the warm weather hits. The romaine is very hardy when it starts to get cold. I start them inside in pots to protect from garden pests when they are tiny and tender and plant them out when they are about 3 inches tall. Since lettuce can only be eaten fresh, grow only about 4 - 8 at a time, depending on how fast you can eat them, and make new starts every 2-3 weeks inside. This way you have fresh salads with sweet young lettuce leaves from April through October, and maybe some romaine into the cold weather months. Some varieties like Mizuna and Arugula can thrive even in the winter months. Choose spinach that is slow to bolt. Spinach can be frozen when you have an over abundance.

Brassicas

This includes cabbage, kale, collards, broccoli, Brussel sprouts and cauliflower. They hold up in cooler weather, but don't really grow and mature unless they get sun and temps in the 70s. They are heavy feeders and like an extra shovel-full of manure at planting time. Broccoli and cauliflower get a sprinkle of bone meal around the roots ends when they first start to flower. They do best when planted 18 - 24 inches apart. You can put in onions, lettuce, spinach, bok choy and carrots in the spaces between and let the large brassica leaves provide shade.

Garlic, Leeks, Onions

I plant garlic bulbs on Jan 1 as a ceremonial act of affirmation for a productive new year. For the last few years, my grandkids have visited for winter holiday and they do the planting. They each get a braid of garlic that they planted when I see them in the summertime.

Many gardeners in my area plant garlic as early as November. I buy organically grown garlic at the market and separate the cloves to go into the ground about 4 inches apart and 3-4 inches deep. I dig trenches for them in late October or November and add bone meal and manure, and sprinkle an inch or two of soil on top, so it will be easier to do the planting in the winter weather. Cover the cloves with 3-4 inches of soil and 3-6 inches of maple leaf or straw mulch. You should start to see sprouts by the end of February and they will be ready to harvest in late June or early July. Give them more chicken manure as a side dressing in May.

I love growing leeks as they feed me year-round. Easy to grow and taste delicious. I buy a 4-inch pot of baby leeks at the garden store, which usually contains dozens of sprouts that can be separated and planted into the garden in March or April. Get the roots very wet before gently separating them and make little holes with your finger or a stick in well manured soil.

Stick them into the ground, pinch or cut o   the tops so that each plant is about 4 inches tall once planted. You will be harvesting from late July to the following spring!

I do not grow bulb onions so you will need to consult elsewhere for that crop. I do put in green (or bunching) onion seeds around other crops to deter garden pests all spring and summer but they don't get used in my kitchen much.

Carrots

This is one of the trickier crops to get started. I usually plant carrot seeds in April. Here is my technique: make sure you have very porous soil at least 8 inches deep. (I use silt from a nearby riverbank, which is better than sand), or lots of potting soil, or vermiculite added to make the soil very light and flu y. Do not add extra manure. Wet the soil deeply before placing seeds. Sprinkle the carrot seeds in rows 3-4 inches apart on top of your specially prepared soil, then cover with fine seed starter soil 1/8-1/4 inch deep over the seeds. Mist with garden hose very gently. Then cover the rows with boards - 1x4 or 2x4s work fine. If it's hot you can water between the rows of boards, but not on top. After about 8 days, start peeking under the boards to see if the little green sprouts are above ground. They can take between 10 and 20 days to sprout. Once the seeds have sprouted, remove the boards and mist daily with the garden hose until they are at least 1 inch tall. You need to thin your carrot rows so plants are 4 inches apart when they get to be 2-3 inches tall. Once established, carrots are easy to grow, don't attract garden pests, and can be kept going for many months, even into the winter. I start a second planting in late June and again in early August for a winter crop.

Beets and Chard

These can be planted directly into the ground in March and on into the summer. Put beet seeds 4-5 inches apart and chard about 18 inches apart. Both of these crops attract a pest called leaf miner in my area so I plant them where I can cover easily with row cover as this is the only way to keep them from being damaged by these pests. More about garden pests in the next section. Beets are long keepers after harvesting, and can be left in the ground through the winter, and dug up, even when there is snow on the ground. Chard also can thrive well into the cold of winter. Carrots, beets and kale actually taste sweeter after they've been through a frost.

Green Beans

Easy to grow, delicious to eat, can be frozen or made into canned dilly beans to add to your winter feasts. I grow the climbing beans since I have limited space, but I've heard that many find they get better production from the bush beans. I build a trellis with 4 8ft tall bamboo poles tied with baling twine at the top, then plant the bottom 4 poles in a 2 foot diameter square pressing the poles at least 4 inches down in the ground. Use skinny 2 - 3 feet long bamboo sticks tied to the bottom about 2-4 inches up the pyramid of upright poles, then use hemp or jute strings going vertically every 2 inches for the beans to grow up. You can soak your bean seeds overnight then plant them an inch down every 2 inches all around your trellis, leaving a foot wide space on the north side, so you can reach in to harvest the beans growing in the middle. You can use the center inside your bean teepee to grow some lettuce or spinach in late summer so it stays cooler.

Beans can be planted as early as April in my area and you will get sweet beans to eat by July, unless it is super hot, which seems to slow the fruiting process. I am guessing you'd get an earlier harvest with bush beans being less affected by the heat, so I am planning to try these this season. Beans, like peas, add nitrogen to the soil so don't need to be fertilized except adding bone meal to the soil before planting. This is one of the easiest and most satisfying crops to grow as they are not susceptible to many garden pests, grow fast, are easy to harvest and yummy to eat, and easy to freeze for winter.

Tomatoes

The most often grown food crop in home gardens! I am so spoiled by the flavors of fresh homegrown tomatoes that I never buy the hard tasteless tomatoes in stores. So I only have fresh tomatoes from mid-July to October, which makes them very precious to me. Pick your warmest sunniest spot for your tomatoes. In my area, they go into the ground in late May as they are very frost sensitive. Plan on about 2- 3 feet of space between plants. I buy local starts about 6-10 inches tall since I've had little success starting from seed (requires very warm soil to germinate). When transplanting, put them down into the ground deep, up to their first leaves, where the stems have little spikes that will turn into more roots.

If you preserve - making sauces or drying - you want to plant some of the Roma variety, as they are more fleshy and easier to peel. For salads, choose the big juicy sweet varieties. I also plant one Sun Gold - the sweetest cherry tomato, which grows very big and productive from July into late October.

Tomatoes are heavy feeders and need strong support systems. If you buy wire cages, bite the bullet and get the sturdiest ones you can find. I use very sturdy bamboo poles 2-3 per cage to try to keep my tomatoes upright as they become heavy with fruit by August. Some gardeners plant steel fence posts in their tomato beds and tie strong wire between to hold up their plants. Since I like to move mine to different spots in the garden from season to season, I have not done this. I pinch off side shoots as they grow to keep the plant producing more tomatoes and less foliage. These shoots that need to be removed grow in the crotch of the main stem and the first branch. I put extra chicken manure and bone meal under and around the plants and try to place them where I can reduce the amount of water they get in late summer. With too much water as they ripen, they can get dry tasteless spots called blossom end rot. If you have only a small space, buy "determinate" varieties which don't grow as big. The ones I've tried are not as sweet and tender as the bigger plants. By August, I am making pasta sauce, dried tomatoes, peeling and freezing bags of tomatoes for brightening winter meals.

Cucumbers

Cucumbers also need warm soil to grow. I start mine inside in April and put them out - 3 plants to a hill - in mid-May. Make a little mound about 18 inches in diameter for each 3 plants. Put a big shovelful of manure under the hill. Build a scaffolding for the plants to grow over so they aren't sitting on the ground, are easier to harvest through the scratchy leaves, and take up less ground space. I like the Persian cukes the best - tender sweet skin, small seeds, crisp and delicious. I find the seeds by googling private growers online. I often grow lemon cukes for their tangy flavor and when picked young, they do not need peeling. And a few pickling cukes. Last year I used the Persian cukes for making pickles and that worked well. Cucumbers need lots of water and plenty of fertilizer also.

Squash and Melons

I don't grow these as I have limited space and they need lots of room - like 3-4 feet diameter for each plant. You need to plant each of these cucurbits distant from one another as they will not cross pollinate and you won't know exactly what you're harvesting. The melons I've tried don't seem to get quite enough sun or heat to get big and sweet. I figure I'm doing my gardening friends a favor to be willing to take their extra zucchinis each summer. If I had more space, I would grow my favorite winter squash, Delicata, for winter feasting.

Corn

Corn needs to be planted at least 3 rows wide in order to be pollinated properly. Bees do the pollinating. This takes up quite a bit of space in your garden. It grows tall so you have to put it where it will not shade your other plants. It is a heavy feeder, requiring extra nitrogen, and uses lots of water. If you have an area that is at least 8 feet square or longer, you can put in a “three sisters” garden with corn, squash and pole green beans. Choose corn varieties that ripen at different times so you don’t find yourself with 2 dozen ears of corn that need to be eaten at the same time. No crop is more delicious than fresh picked corn. If you have too much to eat fresh, you can cut the corn kernels o the cobs and freeze them for winter. Winter squash can feed you throughout the winter months. My favorite for flavor and ease of growing is called Delicata. Excess green beans can easily be frozen or canned.

Basil

I make lots of pesto and so I grow 6-8 basil plants every summer. They are the most frost sensitive, so I buy the starts at the garden store and I put them in the ground in late May/early June. Basil is easy to grow and discourages pests. Just keep clipping off the tops before they go to flower. They will get bushy and you'll have plenty all season. In early October, before the temperature might dip into the low 30s, I dig up one or two basil plants and put them in pots to grow inside in a sunny window in the winter. I do this with parsley also. Plant your baby basils about 8 - 10 inches apart and give them extra manure as a side dressing every month.

Potatoes

I've been growing red and yellow-finn potatoes in old milk crates for a few seasons now, and liking the results. I place a layer of composted leaves on the bottom, a couple inches of garden soil, shovel full of compost, a sprinkling of wood ash from my friend's wood stove, and more garden soil so the layers equal about 4-5 inches, then place small organic potatoes about 4 inches apart on top, then cover with about 3 inches of soil, then top with straw about 4 inches thick. Then water it all in well. Potato leaves are frost sensitive so I start them in April and expect to see some green sprouts coming out the top and sides of planter boxes in May. Keep adding straw as the vines grow taller. Ready to harvest when the vines start to fall down and turn brownish. Don't grow potatoes near your tomatoes. They don't like each other. Although in my kitchen they often appear in the same dish. For a couple of days before harvest, withhold water, then uncover and dig out your new potatoes, brush o the soil and place in shallow baskets or boxes and leave out in the sun to 'cure' for 24 hours. Then brush o all extra soil, and store in a cool dry dark place till you're ready to cook.

Culinary and Medicinal Herbs

Herbs are easy to grow and so very useful in cooking, making teas, repelling garden pests, and many have powerful medicinal properties. Mint adds a wonderful freshness as a garnish for your summer meals and is a delicious tea. It has medicinal properties for digestion and is anti-inflammatory. If you grow it around the perimeter of your house, it discourages rodents. It will spread everywhere by horizontal underground roots unless you keep it in large planter pots. Lemon balm attracts bees, is delightful as a main ingredient in ice tea, has calming effects on the nervous system, discourages pests. It is used to calm restlessness. It is also best in a large pot so it doesn't take over your whole garden.

I start these plants from digging up extra new sprouts in friends' gardens. Comfrey has great medicinal uses. Health benefits of comfrey include its ability to reduce pain and inflammation, boost the immune system, and promote strong bones. It also helps heal skin, and improves respiratory health. It attracts bees. It makes pretty blue flowers which can garnish your summer salads. It has not much flavor but is useful in salves and compresses for healing cuts and bruises. It also spreads wildly so best in large pots. Many organic gardeners like to grow borage, which is also excellent for attracting bees and making pretty blue flowers that can go into your salads. I don't have borage because it takes up too much space in my garden and I don't use it for medicine or cooking.

I also have pots of tarragon, thyme, oregano and chives which can be used fresh or dried in your cooking. Rosemary can grow as a decorative bush. It has anti-inflammatory properties. I use it in cooking roast chicken and lamb. Some say a rosemary plant by your front door protects your home. All these herbs are perennials. They will die back in the winter and magically return the following spring.

I make a medicinal skin salve that uses Cannabis trimmings and Rosemary. It is amazingly useful in reducing pain and inflammation of nerves, muscles and joints. My customers rave about how it helps their arthritic joints and injuries. You can find it for sale on my website: starrbotanicals.com. Perhaps my next book will be about my Cannabis growing tricks.

CREEPY CRAWLIES

The bane of a gardener's life are pests that want to eat your carefully tended plants. These include: hungry birds that will go for your pea sprouts when they are just peeking up out of the ground, snails and slugs, which want to dine on your tender little veggie starts, earwigs, which like everything you grow except herbs, cucumber beetles and leaf miners which can be voracious eaters of your plants, aphids and white flies and cabbage worms which enjoy sucking the liquid from your plant leaves, nematodes, and worst of all, garden symphylans. These are small worms that live in the soil, are 1/4 inch long typically, white or cream, almost translucent in some cases. They look so much like a centipede, that they are frequently called 'garden centipedes.' Garden symphylans thrive best in organic rich, moist soil. They also must have soil that has many worms or at least worm burrows in it, as they travel through the soil in the former burrows of worms or other soil tunneling soil dwellers. Garden symphylans are dangerous to seedlings as they feast on new root growth They attack the new root growth on mature plants as well, and, while they will be unable to kill the plant, they weaken it, which will stunt its growth and make it susceptible to other pests and diseases. They are impossible to get rid of! I had an infestation once and I had to start a whole new garden bed elsewhere as nothing would grow well in that bed. If you are growing in rural areas, you may also be fighting o deer, rabbits, gophers and ground squirrels.

Here's how to win these battles - usually. First, prevention is easier (and cheaper) than the cures. Second, you must watch carefully for early signs of damage and fight back before the pests take over.

Prevention

Your plants will be stronger when you have given them a good foundation by building healthy soil as described - in great detail - above. Second, is creating barriers to these critters: I've had great success using copper tape around my garden beds which is a barrier to slugs and snails. It comes in a roll with paper backing, so all you need to do is peel o the paper backing and stick the copper tape to the frames of your garden beds. I staple it every 3 feet so watering won't remove it. I also use it around tiny plant starts by saving toilet paper rolls, cutting them in half, putting copper tape around and placing them over each lettuce or brassica start as I plant them out in the spring. Press these little guards down into the soil a half inch or so. If you use regular packing tape on the bottom that goes into the ground, they will last several seasons. Tall fences prevent deer problems.

Cures

For snails and earwigs, I resort to a product called SluggoPlus. It really cuts down on the earwig damage and is safe to use around veggies. Sprinkle it around your beds every 2 weeks, and especially in moist dark corners of foliage near your garden, where these pests like to hide out. Works on your flower beds also. Overhead watering dissolves the little pellets so repeat applications are essential. I also use copper tape around my garden beds which works great to keep out snails and slugs.

Cabbage worms are actually the larvae of little white moths that appear usually in July and love your broccoli and other brassicas. You need to watch for the white moths flitting around your plants, then examine the undersides of leaves looking for tiny green worms, nearly the same color as the leaves. They can be 1/4 inch long at first and after feasting on your crop, can get to be 1 inch big. I squish them with my thumb, or if too big for that, drop them into a recycled yogurt cup with wood ash in the bottom. Also good for ending the lives of slugs and snails when you find any that slipped through the copper tape barriers. Many people use little tuna cans or yogurt cups half filled with soy sauce and vegetable oil to lure and then trap earwigs. You place them a couple inches deep all around your veggies. I have also heard of rolling up damp newspaper and leaving near your veggies to trap earwigs, but this has never worked for me. The containers of soy and oil will need to be replaced after each watering as they get filled with water and thousands of earwigs. That's why I end up each season using SluggoPlus. I am finding sprinkling diatomaceous earth on my brassicas is working well to keep down aphids, white flies and cabbage worms. It is inexpensive and easy to use and good for the plants and soil.

The only way I have succeeded in keeping leaf miner larvae from burrowing into the leaves of beets and chard, is to cover the plants early on with Row Cover or screens. You know you have leaf miner when you see white/gray lines and patches in the leaves of the plants. Remove any leaves that have this damage, then cover with row cover or screens. Use 2x4s or rocks to hold the edges of the row cover down, so the bugs are not able to sneak in.

Aphids usually appear in later summer. Lady bugs love to eat aphids, so you need to acquire these from your garden store and release them when you see first signs of these tiny pale green bugs sucking the juices from the center tender leaves of your brassicas. I also use strong streams of hose water to remove most of the aphids.

I use yellow sticky cards hung above and around plants that show signs of white flies. Neither of these methods work great, but you can keep the bug population down enough to keep your plants going at the end of the growing season. Squash bugs look like yellow ladybugs with black stripes. They go for cucumber, squash and melon leaves. I squish them with my fingers when I see them, but they are fast and know how to drop to the ground and hide in the mulch when they see you coming. I have never had much damage from these, so they are not at the top of my garden enemy list.

My best years for minimizing bug and slug damage was when I had ducks in my garden. They went after all these garden pests and did not eat the veggies. They will trample baby plants so you have to protect the new plants from the waddlers.

I have had root damage from ground squirrels and gophers. It can be shocking to walk out to your garden and find your 2-3 foot tall broccoli lying on the ground, detached from their roots completely. Or a row of carrots turned into holes in the ground where they grew happily the day before. For these pests, I've had

immediate success using something called Wolf Pee Pellets. Smells absolutely disgusting! Says it works on rabbits and moles as well. Get it from your local garden store, or (shamefully) found it on Amazon, as soon as you see damage, sprinkle it in any holes and around plants you want to protect. Perfectly safe for your veggies and works very quickly to repel these creatures. Use about once a week after watering to be sure these destructive critters have moved elsewhere.

I've never had to deal with rabbits or deer. Deer can leap over 6 foot fences, I've been told, so if you know there are deer in your area, you must have fencing with wire going up 7 - 8 feet. If you can't build such a fence, there is liquid deer repellent that you need to spray all around the perimeter of your garden every few days. In my big rural garden, I used bedding I got from a wild animal sanctuary nearby that kept lions and tigers! Deer never entered that garden even 6 years later.

Beneficial Critters

By now you probably realize that some critters in your garden are your good friends. Earthworms are especially precious as they feed your soil and aerate it with their tunnels. Soil teeming with earthworms is healthy soil that produces happy veggies. Ladybugs eat aphids to keep your brassicas happy. Bees, butterflies and dragonflies are essential pollinators for your garden plants. So don't put poison in your soil or on your plants that could harm these important helpers.

I hope these battles against pests don't discourage you from starting out as a first-time food grower. Remember this is just a part of every gardener's repertoire, and build it into your plan from the start. Ask other growers in your area what has worked for them, sharing experiences is a great help. Expect to lose some plants to critters, learn to grow what works best in your area, and be sure to plant in soil that is as healthy and fertile as you can make it. The key to keeping pests at bay is constant diligence. I go out and wander through the garden nearly every morning, usually barefooted, and just take in what I see and feel there. It actually feels like the plants speak to me and tell me what they need that day.

WINTER GROWING

Several crops do well in cold weather, so with some planning, you can be eating from your garden year-round.

In S. Oregon, you need to start your winter veggies in pots indoors in late July or early August! They need to be well established by mid-September when the weather starts to turn cooler. As mentioned before, the leeks I plant out in March or April are still feeding me a year later. Romaine lettuce is winter hardy as is kale, some broccoli varieties, Brussel sprouts, collards, chard, beets and carrots. It is so satisfying to brave the cold wet weather in February to gather fresh kale, collards and leeks for your winter soups and casseroles!

TO SUMMARIZE

All this is a lot of information to take in. Don't be overwhelmed. It's one little task at a time. Please know that once your garden is established, you will need to spend less than an hour maximum every other day doing garden tasks - including planting, watering, weeding, compost turning, harvesting and dealing with pest issues. Getting started from scratch, plan on

1 - 2 hours every day for a week or two to get things going. I know some gardeners who go out and do all their planting and building of beds and trellises, mixing of soil in one or two weekends, but that is not at all necessary. You can decide to grow three or four crops in one raised bed the first season. Start your seeds indoors in Feb/March/April. Get your beds set up, filled with soil and amendments over several days before your plants are ready to go out, plant and set up a watering system a week or so later, and just be leisurely about the whole project. Keep track of the weather predictions and set out your plants when it will be above 40 degrees and not windy or pouring rain. If a surprise cold spell comes along after your plants are in the ground, keep a roll of row cover nearby and cover your plants that night.

You will quickly learn what parts of food growing you enjoy most, and focus on that at first. If you like standing outside barefooted, watering your plants by hand, do that while communing with the plants and letting them tell you what they need next. Get help from friends when you decide to construct a new bed, and fill it with good fertile soil. Get your compost bin going in the Fall, plant in April or May; just take it slow and let it be something you enjoy doing. Welcome the challenges as opportunities to be creative, resourceful, and to learn from other gardeners. Know you are setting an example for your friends and neighbors to follow in your footsteps.

Okay, probably nobody enjoys fighting off garden pests, but usually they won't be a problem till you are well into the fun parts. And the best is, of course, the joy of harvesting tasty, healthy food to share with family and friends. Finally, there is the deep satisfaction of knowing you did your part to free yourself somewhat from corporate control of your food supply.

Happy Gardening, friends.

www.ingramcontent.com/pod-product-compliance
Lightning Source LLC
LaVergne TN
LVHW050542100826
845148LV00002B/649
* 9 7 8 1 7 3 6 6 4 1 1 4 9 *